DATE DUE

CHECKERBOARD HOW-TO LIBRARY

COOL ART

COOL COLLAGE

THE ART OF CREATIVITY
FOR KIDS!

ANDERS HANSON

ABDO
Publishing Company

CONTENTS

Published by ABDO Publishing Company, 8000 West 78th Street, Edina, Minnesota 55439.

Copyright © 2009 by Abdo Consulting Group, Inc. International copyrights reserved in all countries.

No part of this book may be reproduced in any form without written permission from the publisher. Checkerboard Library™ is a trademark and logo of ABDO Publishing Company.

Printed in the United States.

Editor: Pam Price

Series Concept: Nancy Tuminelly

Cover and Interior Design: Anders Hanson, Mighty Media

Photo Credits: Anders Hanson, Shutterstock

Library of Congress Cataloging-in-Publication Data

Hanson, Anders, 1980-

Cool collage : the art of creativity for kids / Anders Hanson.

   p. cm. -- (Cool art)

Includes index.

ISBN 978-1-60453-146-6

1. Collage--Technique--Juvenile literature. I. Title.

N7433.7.H36 2008

702.81'2--dc22

2008008641

Get the Picture!

When a step number in an activity has a colored circle around it, look for the picture that goes with it. The picture's border will be the same color as the circle.

THE ART OF creativity

You Are Creative

Being creative is all about using your imagination to make new things. Coming up with new ideas and bringing them to life is part of being human. Everybody is creative! Creative thinking takes time and practice. But that's okay, because being creative is a lot of fun!

Calling All Artists

Maybe you believe that you aren't good at art. Maybe you have some skills that you want to improve. The purpose of this book is to help you develop your visual creativity. Remember that your artistic skills improve every time you make art. The activities in this book can help you become the creative artist you want to be!

Creativity Tips

- Stay positive.
- There is no wrong way to be creative.
- Allow yourself to make mistakes.
- Tracing isn't cheating.
- Practice, practice, practice.
- Be patient.
- Have fun!

COLLAGE IS COOL!

... the principle of collage is the central principle of all art
in the twentieth century. —Donald Barthelme

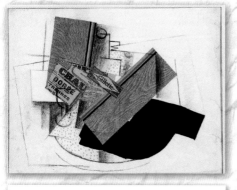
STILL LIFE ON A TABLE: GILLETTE (1914)
— GEORGES BRAQUE

What Is Collage?

The word *collage* comes from the French word *coller*, which means "to glue." Artists who create collages are called collagists. They create art by gluing papers or small objects to a flat surface.

Collage has been around for thousands of years. But until 1912, most people didn't think of it as art. That year, two famous painters, Pablo Picasso and Georges Braque, began gluing scraps of paper to their canvases.

The Birth of an Art Form

Picasso and Braque were interested in expanding the bounds of art. They felt that **traditional** forms of art, such as drawing and painting, were too limited. They sought a new medium for expressing themselves. They found it in printed papers.

In the 19th century, faster printing presses were made. This led to a dramatic increase in printed papers. By the early 20th century, printed newspapers and ads were everywhere. Picasso and Braque saw this as a chance to create art in a new way.

Picasso and Braque cut words and pictures out of newspapers. They saw patterns they liked in wallpaper and used those too. They took everyday prints out of their usual settings and used them in works of art. In a way, they took the ordinary and transformed it into the extraordinary. In the process, they introduced the world to a new form of **fine art**.

Be a Collagist!

Learning to collage is easy and fun! It's easy because all you need is glue, scissors, paper scraps, and a base. It's fun because you can do anything that your imagination comes up with!

If you are not satisfied with your first collages, remember this. Great artists are not always satisfied with their work. Part of what makes them great is that they are always trying to get better. You don't need to be good at art now to become a great artist. You just need the desire to learn and become better!

GLASS AND BOTTLE OF SUZE (1912)
— PABLO PICASSO

Don't Be a Judge!

When discussing a work of art, avoid using the words listed below. They offer judgments without saying much about the character of the work. Instead, look at how the artist used composition and **techniques**. Try to understand what the artist was trying to achieve. See pages 8 through 13 to read about these elements.

- good
- bad
- right
- wrong
- silly
- stupid

Have Patience

Be patient with yourself. Changes won't happen overnight. When you do a collage you don't like, don't throw it out. Save it so you can look back later and see how much you've improved! Have **confidence** in yourself. You can do anything you set your mind to!

5

TOOLS OF THE TRADE

BRUSH

SAND

TAGBOARD

FOAM CORE

SCISSORS

PIPE CLEANERS

PENCIL

WHITE PENCIL

PEN

OLD MAGAZINES

6

Each activity in this book has a list of the tools and materials you will need. When you come across a tool you don't know, turn back to this page. You can find most of these items at your local art store.

GLUE STICK

FELT

PASTE

PAPER GLUE

COLORED CARD STOCK
OR CONSTRUCTION PAPER

MARTHA STEWART

YOU HAVE
$6,000 HIDDEN AWAY!
Suze Orman
Helps You Find It

Basic Elements

These are the elements that make up images. All collages can be described by these key **concepts**.

Point

Glue a small object, such as a bead or a seed, to your base to create a point.

Line

Apply long, thin objects to your base to create lines. For example, you can make lines with twigs, pipe cleaners, wire, toothpicks, or yarn.

Shape

In collage, shapes are usually created with pieces of cut paper or cloth. Large found objects, such as leaves, flowers, and feathers, also create shapes.

Pattern

Some papers and fabrics have printed patterns. Wallpaper and clothing are often patterned. You can also arrange found objects to create patterns.

Texture

In collage, texture is often something you can feel. Crinkled tissue paper, sand, handmade paper, and rice are a few items that create texture.

Value

Value describes how light or dark an element is. Light objects have little value. Dark objects have a lot of value.

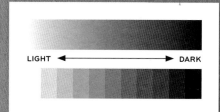

LIGHT ← → DARK

Color

To add color, simply choose elements that have the color you're looking for. You can also paint objects before or after you glue them down.

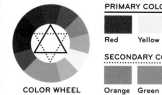

COLOR WHEEL

PRIMARY COLORS
Red   Yellow   Blue

SECONDARY COLORS
Orange   Green   Violet

Composition

Bringing together the basic elements to make a work of art is called composition. The following ideas will help you create great compositions!

Focal Point

The focal point is the first thing you see when you look at a collage. Without a focal point, a collage may seem **chaotic**.

FOCUSED

UNFOCUSED

Balance

Balance refers to the arrangement of elements in a collage. Evenly spread objects create balance. Objects grouped in one area create an unbalanced composition.

BALANCED

UNBALANCED

Movement

Movement occurs when things appear to be traveling across a collage. The image on the left moves like a river. The one on the right feels calm, like a lake.

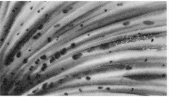

MOVEMENT

STILLNESS

Space

Whenever an object is glued to a base, two shapes are made. The shape of the object is called positive space. The shape outside the object is called negative space. When these shapes work well together, the composition is more interesting.

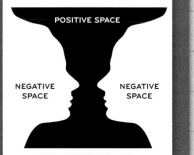

POSITIVE SPACE

NEGATIVE SPACE

NEGATIVE SPACE

Rhythm

Rhythm isn't just for musicians! Repeating an element many times gives the work a feeling of rhythm.

RHYTHMIC LINES

Harmony

When two or more elements in a collage share **characteristics**, they are in **harmony**. When elements don't have much in common, they are **dissonant**. Characteristics that help create harmony include color, size, and shape.

HARMONIC SHAPES

DISSONANT SHAPES

Contrast

Contrast occurs when art has both extremes of an element. Using smooth and rough textures, light and dark values, or large and small shapes are ways to add contrast.

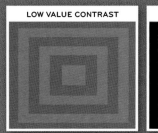

LOW VALUE CONTRAST

HIGH VALUE CONTRAST

Techniques

Artists use various **techniques** to create the elements of a collage.
Get out some collage tools and try these techniques as you read about them.

Cutting

Use scissors to cut lightweight papers and fabrics. Always cut away from your body. Watch out for your fingers! If you have trouble cutting something, ask an adult for help.

Tearing

Tearing produces a jagged edge. Wet paper is easier to tear than dry paper. You can use a waterlogged brush to "paint" a tear line. This helps control where the paper will tear.

Gluing

Using the right amount of glue and applying it well are important skills. Beginning collagists tend to use too much glue. A thin layer of glue is usually all you need.

Choose a tool to apply the glue with. Cotton balls or folded paper towels work well. You can use brushes to apply some glues. Clean the brushes thoroughly after each use. Rub the bristles between your fingers while running warm water over them. Work soap into the bristles until they're clean. Rinse and dry with a paper towel.

Place the object to be glued on a paper towel. Spread the glue to the edges, including any corners. Carefully place the material in the desired spot. Use your finger or the back of a spoon to rub the object into the base. Start at the center and work your way to the edges.

Types of Glue

- Yes Paste is popular because it doesn't wrinkle paper.

- Glue sticks are good for lightweight papers.

- Zip Dry and Sobo glues are good for attaching heavy objects.

- Don't use rubber cement because it has chemicals that can damage paper.

A Strong Base

Choosing the right base for your collage is important. If the base is too thin, it won't support the materials you glue to it. So, don't use printer paper. Use one of these materials instead.

- card stock
- cardboard
- foam core
- tagboard

- watercolor paper
- wood

FUNNY FACES
Create wacky characters from cutouts!

Stuff You'll Need
Magazine cutouts or photos of faces, scissors, glue, base

1. Look through magazines for pictures of human and animal faces. It's even more fun to use pictures of family, friends, and pets. Just make sure it's okay to cut up the pictures. The faces should be large and easy to see.

2. Leave one face whole. You will glue parts of other faces on top of this face. Cut the other faces into parts. Cut out the nose of one face and the mouth of another. Use both eyes from one face, or choose eyes from different faces. Ears, hair, facial hair, and hats are other fun parts you can include.

3. Arrange the face parts on top of the whole face. When you get a good laugh out of it, you'll know you're on the right track!

4. Are you satisfied with your composition? Then glue down the images you've chosen!

PUPPY LOVE

Circles and ovals team up to make this cute pooch!

More Animals to Make

Stuff You'll Need

Colored construction paper, scissors, glue, base, felt, buttons, pipe cleaners

16

1. Cut two ovals from a sheet of colored paper. One should be larger than the other.

2. Glue the small oval to your base. Position the large oval so it covers the top part of the small oval. Glue it in place.

3. Cut two smaller ovals from white felt. Glue these side by side in the upper middle of the large oval.

4. Cut a small oval of pink paper. Then cut it in half crosswise. Glue it so that it overlaps the bottom edge of the large oval. The round end should point down.

5. Choose a colored paper that's a little darker than the first color. Cut a circle for the belly, two ovals for the ears, and two tiny ovals for the feet. Glue these down.

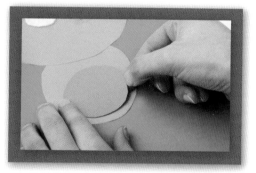

6. Cut an oval for the snout. It should fit below the eyes and overlap the top of the pink shape. Cut a small triangular shape out of the bottom of the snout. Glue it down.

7. Find a large black button for the nose and two small buttons for the eyes. Attach them with Zip Dry or Sobo glue.

8. Cut and bend a short piece of pipe cleaner for the tail. Glue it next to the body.

WACKY WINDOWS

Decorate your windows with see-through fun!

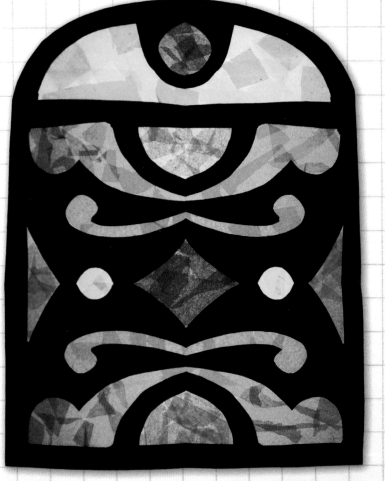

Stained Glass

This project is designed to look like a stained glass window. When light shines through it, the colors come to life!

Stuff You'll Need

Black construction paper, scissors, white pencil, colored tissue paper, paper towels, glue stick

1. Set a sheet of black construction paper in front of you. Position the paper vertically so it is taller than it is wide.

2. Fold the paper in half lengthwise.

3. Draw a line across the paper about 2 to 3 inches (5 to 7 cm) from the top.

4. Bring the bottom edge of the paper up to this line. Crease the fold.

5. Draw a curved line from the top left corner to the right end of the first line you drew. Cut along the curved line.

6. Now it's time to cut away shapes. But first, look at the photo on the left. Do not cut or remove the areas shaded with white lines. You can draw these areas on your paper too. They're about a half inch (1.3 cm) wide.

7. Use the scissors to cut away any kind of shapes you like. Leave about a half inch (1.3 cm) of paper between shapes. The photo on the right shows how the example looked before it was unfolded.

8 When you're done cutting, unfold your paper. Trace each shape onto a different color of tissue paper. Cut out the traced shapes. But don't cut on the lines. Instead, cut outside them. Leave about a quarter inch (0.6 cm) between your scissors and the traced outlines.

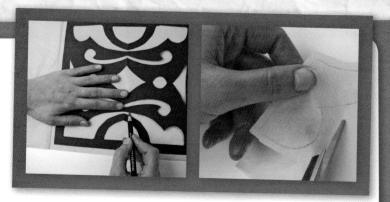

9 Cover your workspace in paper towels. Use the glue stick to apply glue to the edges of a cutout area. Move the artwork to a different section of the paper towel.

10 Get the piece of tissue paper that matches that shape. Place the tissue paper on top of the cutout so that all of its edges are glued.

11 Repeat steps 9 and 10 until all of the shapes are filled with tissue paper.

12 Tear small pieces of tissue paper and glue them to the back of each shape. These pieces should be the same color as the shape that they're glued to.

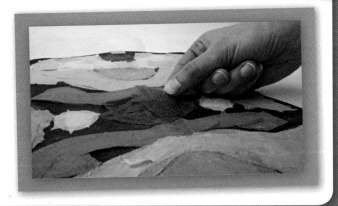

13 Allow your art to dry. Then tape it to a window.

SAND AND SURF

Use your imagination to create beautiful beaches!

Stuff You'll Need

Base, pencil, colored tissue paper, glue, scissors, sand

1   Use a sheet of white tagboard, foam core, or watercolor paper for your base. Position the base horizontally so that it's wider than it is tall. Lightly draw a horizontal line across the middle of the base. This is called a horizon line. It separates the sky from the earth.

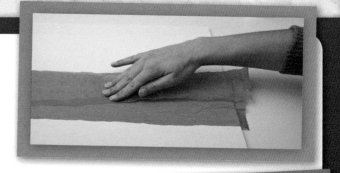

2   Tear some strips of dark blue, blue, and orange tissue paper. Make the strips a little longer than your base. They should be about 1 to 2 inches (2.5 to 5 cm) wide.

3   Start with the orange strips. Glue them along the horizon line. Overlap them a little bit so the horizon line is covered up.

4   Now glue a dark blue strip to the top of the base.

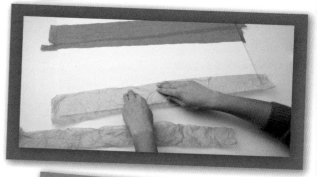

5   Glue two strips of blue to the bottom of your base. They should overlap each other.

6   Tear some yellow strips. Glue one between the bottom of the base and the horizon line. Glue the other between the horizon line and the top.

7 Now tear two light pink strips. Make them about an inch (2.5 cm) wider than the spaces between the yellow and orange strips. Glue them down so they slightly overlap the yellow and orange strips.

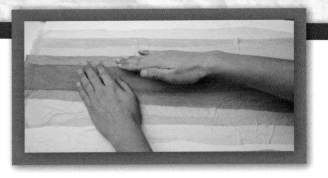

8 Finally, cover the rest of your base with light blue strips.

9 Tear a long mountain shape from dark tissue paper. Use the scissors to cut a straight edge along the bottom edge of the mountain. Place it along the horizon line and glue it down.

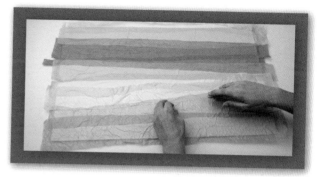

10 Try to tear a similar shape for the mountain's reflection. It can be a different color from the mountain. But it should still be dark. Cut off the top part with a scissors. Glue it just below the mountain.

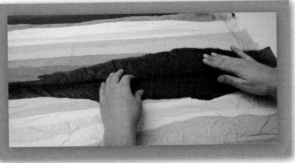

11 Get out the sand. Using a cotton ball, apply glue along the bottom edge of the base.

12 Sprinkle sand over the glue until it's completely covered. Take the collage outside or to a wastebasket to shake off any excess sand.

POP-UP CARD

Make a creative card to let someone know you care!

Stuff You'll Need

Colored card stock, scissors, glue, pen (optional),
string (optional), ribbon (optional), white pencil (optional)

1. Choose a piece of colored card stock for the base. Cut it to measure 7 inches by 10 inches (17.8 cm by 25.4 cm). Fold this piece of paper in half crosswise to make a card.

2. Draw two parallel lines down from the folded edge of the card. Each one should be one inch (2.5 cm) long and one inch (2.5 cm) away from the side of the card. Cut along these lines.

3. Fold back and crease the section between the cuts.

4. Open the card like a tent. Push the folded section down into the inside of the card. Close the card firmly.

5. Choose a different color for the background. Cut a piece that is 6 inches by 9 inches (15.2 cm by 22.9 cm). Fold it in half crosswise and open it again. Apply glue along the edges only. Lay the card with the outside facing up. Center the background on the card and glue it in place.

6 Open the card. There should now be a section that sticks out from the middle of the card. This is the pop-up holder.

7 Now it's time to create the pop-up. The example card has a birthday cake. But you can make anything you want! The pop-up piece should be no taller than 4 inches (10.2 cm) and no wider than 5 inches (12.7 cm).

8 Apply glue to the bottom side of the pop-up holder. Press the pop-up piece against the pop-up holder. Allow it to dry.

9 Decide what you want on the front of your card. The example has a present made of card stock and string. It's also decorated with ribbon and the words *happy birthday*. Lightweight decorations such as fabric, beads, and yarn also work well.

10 Find or create the elements you want and glue them to the front of the card.

COLLAGE BATTLE

Monster and machine duke it out in space!

Stuff You'll Need
Lots of magazines, scissors, glue, base

1 Look through magazines for images of the sky or outer space. You can also use images of things that look like space, such as underwater photos. Can you see the sea turtle in the upper left corner of the example? All the images should have some blue in them.

2 Cut out the images. Arrange them on the upper part of your base. Glue them down.

3 Find some images of land. Or look for things that look like land, such as rocks, grass, and trees. Cut them out. Arrange these pictures on the bottom part of your base. The entire base should now be filled with images. Glue the images to the base.

4 Now look for images of machines and metal things. Imagine how these things could become parts of a robot body. In the example shown, an old telephone is the head. The front of a truck is the chest. The left shoulder is an old microphone.

5 Cut out these images and arrange them in the shape of a robot. What kind of robot do you want to make? Does it have legs or wheels? How about arms? Rearrange your images until you're happy with the robot. Then glue down the images on the right side of your base.

6 Now it's time to make your monster. Look through magazines to find images of nature. Most of these images should be green. Reptile and bird parts are great for monster making. The example has an alligator head, a parrot wing, vulture feet, a chameleon tail, and an iguana body. Its eye is a ladybug, and it has leaves that look like spikes.

7 Arrange the nature images in the shape of a monster. Glue them down on the left side of your base, facing the robot. And you're done!

What's next?

Taking Care of Your Collages

Caring for collages can be tricky. Three-dimensional objects glued to your base can easily be knocked off. Flat collages can sometimes fray. Use the tips below to help protect your art.

- Strong, stiff materials make the best bases. This is especially true when a collage includes heavy objects. Lightweight bases may tear or crumple if they are stressed by too much weight.

- You might want to buy a cardboard portfolio to keep flat collages in. You can find one at any art store. And, they actually work better than the expensive leather portfolios!

- Put sheets of newsprint or extra sheets of paper between the collages in your portfolio. This will prevent them from rubbing against each other.

Try Something New!

The activities in this book are just a few examples of fun collage projects you can do. Once you've completed them all, try some of the projects again with different materials or subjects. Then make up some projects of your own!

Collecting Materials

Collagists are always looking for stuff to make art with. If you build a collection of cool things, you can collage anytime. Start by creating a special place to keep collage materials. A simple folder works great for paper finds. Small plastic drawers organize other materials well.

GLOSSARY

chaotic – of or relating to a state of total confusion.

characteristic – a quality or a feature of something.

concept – an idea.

confidence – a feeling of faith in your own abilities.

dissonant – having parts that don't go well together.

fine art – art that focuses on the creation of beautiful objects.

harmony – going or working well together.

technique – a method or style in which something is done.

traditional – based on a usual or customary behavior, thought, style, or action passed from one generation to the next.

Web Sites

To learn more about cool art, visit ABDO Publishing Company on the World Wide Web at **www.abdopublishing.com**. Web sites about cool art are featured on our Book Links page. These links are routinely monitored and updated to provide the most current information available.